A Look through the
Mouse Hole

A Look through the Mouse Hole

by Heiderose and Andreas Fischer-Nagel

A Carolrhoda Nature Watch Book

Carolrhoda Books, Inc./Minneapolis

*Many thanks to Evan B. Hazard, Ph.D., Professor
of Biology, Bemidji State University, for his assistance.
Dr. Hazard is the author of* Mammals of Minnesota.

To our children, Tamarica and Cosmea Désirée

This edition first published 1989 by Carolrhoda Books, Inc.
Original edition copyright © 1986 by Kinderbuchverlag KBV Luzern AG,
Lucerne, Switzerland, under the title BLICK DURCHS MAUSELOCH.
Translated from the German by Gerd Kirchner.
Adapted by Carolrhoda Books, Inc.

All additional material supplied for this edition ©1989 by
Carolrhoda Books, Inc.

LIBRARY OF CONGRESS CATALOGING-IN-PUBLICATION DATA

Fischer-Nagel, Heiderose.
  [Blick durchs Mauseloch. English]
  A look through the mouse hole / by Heiderose and Andreas
Fischer-Nagel.
        p.   cm.
  "A Carolrhoda nature watch book."
  Translation of: Blick durchs Mauseloch.
  Includes index.
  Summary: Photographs and text observe the behavior of a family of
mice living in a basement, comparing their habits to those of
outdoor mice. Includes information on the care of pet mice.
  ISBN 0-87614-326-5
  1. Mice—Juvenile literature. 2. Mice as pets—Juvenile
literature. 3. Household ecology—Juvenile literature. [1. Mice]
I. Fischer-Nagel, Andreas. II. Title.
QL737.R638F5213   1989
599.32′33—dc19   88-39639
                                                      CIP
                                                       AC

Manufactured in the United States of America

1 2 3 4 5 6 7 8 9 10 99 98 97 96 95 94 93 92 91 90 89

No matter where you live, you may one day be surprised by a tiny grayish brown animal scampering across your kitchen or basement. This little creature is *Mus musculus,* the house mouse.

Ever since people started to grow grain, about 8,000 years ago, house mice have depended on us for food and shelter. The mice quickly discovered that it was easier to eat people's food than to gather their own, and human shelters protected them from predators and bad weather.

Not all house mice live in houses. Many live in barns, garages, or fields— wherever they can easily find people's food supplies. Some house mice live outdoors during spring and summer, and indoors during fall and winter.

House mice probably first lived in the dry parts of central Asia. From there, they spread to Europe and were carried around the world on ships as stowaways. Wherever people's food went, from ships to land, *Mus musculus* went too.

One evening, we heard a soft rustling sound coming from our basement. We crept quietly downstairs and discovered two tiny creatures sitting in a corner, nibbling at some food. We were sharing our house with a pair of house mice.

House mice usually have grayish brown fur that fades to a paler yellow brown on their underbodies. Their scaly tails also have a light covering of hair. Eyes like shiny black beads peer out over pointed noses and long, quivering whiskers. When fully grown, their bodies and tails are each 3 to 4 inches (7-10 cm) long. House mice are only about 1 inch (2.5 cm) tall at the shoulder and weigh less than 1 ounce (28 g).

We wanted to learn more about the mice who had moved into our house, so we settled down to watch them.

Although the mice in our basement appeared to live alone, house mice usually live in extended families, or **colonies**. Each colony establishes its **territory** and marks boundaries with urine and droppings. This marking causes the musty smell people notice wherever mice are living. If a mouse enters another colony's territory, it will be recognized as an intruder and chased away.

A female house mouse is **in heat**, or ready to mate, every three to six days. Before mating, the male mouse chases the female. He licks and sniffs her. The female then pulls her tail a little to the side and stretches her hindquarters up so the male can reach them from behind. The male mounts the female and deposits his **sperm**, or male reproductive cells, inside of her.

At first, we didn't know whether our mice were male or female, because it is very difficult to tell the sexes apart without picking them up. We soon learned that one was male and one was female when we saw them mating. We decided to call them Fiona and Franz.

Soon after mating, Fiona began to gather nesting material. There was plenty of straw, cardboard, and paper in our basement, but Fiona found something better upstairs—a laundry basket filled with socks.

House mice build their nests from shredded bits of the softest, warmest materials they can find. Outdoor house mice usually have nests made of feathers, fur, leaves, grass, straw, or hay. Indoor house mice have even more materials to choose from.

Fiona pulled a soft red sock out of the basket and quickly dragged it through a mouse hole and back to the basement.

Newborn mice need a nest temperature of about 86°F (30°C). If the temperature drops below this, the mother mouse will add another layer to the nest. For extra warmth, outdoor mice will often build their nests in **burrows**, or holes they have dug in the ground.

If the nest temperature falls below 50°F (10°C), the female mouse will move to a new warmer location.

Sometimes, several females in a colony of house mice will share a nest. They help raise each other's young and will even feed each other's offspring. These shared nests do not need to be as thick as other nests because of the warmth of all the little bodies.

About three weeks after mating, a house mouse has from 4 to 13 **pups**, or baby mice. A litter of 7 is about average. The mother mouse squats and presses out one pup after another. Each mouse is born encased in an **amniotic sac** and is attached to its mother by an **umbilical cord**. With her teeth, the mother rips the sac open and bites through the cord. Then she licks her new baby until it is clean and dry. Usually, within half an hour, all the baby mice are born and are nursing at their mother's **teats,** or nipples.

The birth usually occurs at night when darkness makes the mother feel safest. If a mother house mouse is disturbed while giving birth, she may panic and eat some, or all, of her pups.

At birth, a baby house mouse is pink and has no hair—only whiskers. It is only about 1/2 inch (1.3 cm) long including its tail and weighs less than 1/25 ounce (about 1 g). At first, its eyes and ears are tightly closed, and its toes are fused together. Baby mice are **altricial**, which means they are born completely helpless. Animals that are more independent at birth, such as ducks, deer, and horses, are **precocial**.

15

If for any reason the mother thinks that her nest is not safe, she will move her young to another nest. When she picks them up, the young mice become very stiff, which makes them easy to carry. It takes a few seconds after the pups are put down for this "carrying rigidity" to wear off.

Baby mice are helpless at first, but they develop very quickly. On the 2nd or 3rd day of life, hair begins to grow in dark patches on their heads and backs. The hair soon spreads across their sides to their bellies.

By the 4th or 5th day, the pups' eyes are still closed, but their ears are open, and their toes have separated. Near the 8th day, the tiny mice, still totally blind, make their first clumsy attempts at walking on wobbly legs. By the 10th day, the baby mice are covered with fur and look quite different from the tiny pink creatures they were at birth.

Sometime between the 13th and 15th day, the young mice open their eyes and look curiously at their surroundings for the first time. Before long, they will be ready to explore the world beyond their nest.

By the time the mice are 17 days old, they can nibble solid food. At three weeks, young mice can eat and drink on their own, but the mother doesn't **wean** them until they're about a month old.

The mother mouse keeps her nest clean and her offspring well groomed. But this is not just the chore of a mother mouse. Adult mice in a colony spend hours every day grooming each other, especially hard-to-reach places like necks and backs.

The mother mouse is also fiercely protective and will defend her offspring against enemies many times her size— even dogs, cats, and humans. She will shield her pups with her body or jump at the enemy with teeth bared, risking her life to defend her young.

The father mouse does not take care of the young mice as the mother does. His main role is to protect his family from strange mice venturing into his territory.

A **hierarchy**, or chain of command, exists among the male mice in a colony. If a colony is small, it is divided into smaller territories, each guarded by a male mouse with one or two mates. If the colony grows too large, however, it will have only one male leader, the **chief buck**.

The chief buck—usually an older male—is the strongest mouse in the colony. He is the only male allowed to mate, so the colony grows more slowly. Any male may challenge the chief buck by starting a fight. If the chief buck is defeated, the colony gets a new, usually younger, leader.

When the young mice are four weeks old, the mother and father introduce them to their home territory. House mice are most active at night. One evening, we saw several tiny noses poking out of the basement nest, sniffing excitedly left and right.

Gradually, the little mice crawled out and explored the basement. House mice can only see a few inches in front of their faces, and they can't see details. But they can see the movement of an enemy approaching from almost any direction because of the shape and position of their bulging eyes.

What house mice lack in eyesight, they make up for in their keenest sense, that of smell. Their noses warn them of enemies, help them locate food, and guide them around their territories.

As they move, a scented oily substance is released from glands in the soles of their feet. By smelling the trails left by this substance, house mice can not only find their way around their territories, but they can also tell if outsiders have crossed their boundaries.

The hearing of house mice is also extraordinary. Their large ears are exceptionally sensitive to high-pitched sounds. Most of the squeaking noises that mice make to communicate are too high for human ears to hear.

The long, quivering whiskers, or **tactile hairs,** provide house mice with an additional sense of touch. Not only do they have these special hairs around their mouths and noses, and above their eyes, but they also have them on the sides of their bodies and the outsides of their legs.

To survive, house mice must be able to hide quickly from their enemies, so they depend on dark, narrow spaces and passageways. Many house mice are saved by their whiskers. In a split second, the whiskers let the mice know if tiny openings are big enough for their bodies.

As we watched the young mice, it seemed there was no place they could not go. House mice have an excellent sense of balance. Using their long tails to steady themselves, they climb thin ropes, jump long distances, and even swim if they have to. One night, Fiona and Franz led their pups up through the walls of our house and into the kitchen, where they could investigate our food supplies.

Whether house mice live indoors or outdoors, they will probably steal food from people. The word *mouse* comes from the ancient Sanskrit word *mus*, which means *thief*. For outdoor house mice, this may mean raiding a barn or silo, or living on the grain growing in a farmer's field. Grain is one of their favorite foods. Outdoor house mice can also live on wild plants and even eat insects.

Every year, as winter approaches, outdoor house mice must **hoard** food for the long months ahead. If the temperature drops too low and food becomes too scarce, outdoor house mice may temporarily move into human shelters.

House mice can also survive in an underground burrow by falling into a deep sleep called **dormancy**. At first glance, a dormant mouse may appear to be dead. Its body has stiffened as its temperature has dropped. Its heartbeat and other body functions have slowed down to use less energy.

Indoor house mice do not have to work as hard for their food as do outdoor house mice. They generally do not hoard food because they can usually find plenty of it in any season. Almost anything house mice can steal from their human hosts is fair game. They like cereal, pasta, and other grain products; meat, cheese, and peanut butter. Sometimes they will eat fruits and vegetables, although these are not their favorite foods. Mice will even gnaw on such things as wood, leather, glue, soap, candles, and plaster.

House mice can do a lot of damage in their search for food. Although they eat very little per day, about 1/10 ounce (3 g), they can destroy great amounts of food. Nibbling a little of this and a little of that, they leave food strewn all over. They also have the unpleasant habit of leaving urine and droppings wherever they eat. This spoils even the food they leave behind.

When you share a house with mice, it is very difficult to keep them from getting into your food. They can chew their way through almost any barrier and into almost any container. They are members of the order of mammals called *Rodentia,* commonly known as **rodents.** One feature that makes rodents different from most other mammals is their large front teeth, or **incisors**, which never stop growing. By constantly gnawing on things, rodents wear these teeth down so they don't get too long. This also makes their incisors razor sharp.

Indoor house mice may seem to have an easy life, but they do have to beware of some enemies. Most people prefer not to have mice in their homes, so they set traps to catch them. This house mouse is lucky because it got caught in a live trap, rather than in one that would have killed it. This mouse will be taken far away from the house and set free.

Indoor mice also have to be wary of household pets. Cats are especially skillful and patient mouse catchers. They will crouch for hours in front of a mouse hole without moving. And, as many careless mice have discovered, cats may lurk outdoors as well as indoors.

Outdoor house mice face even more dangers than indoor house mice do. The red fox, one of nature's best mouse catchers, prowls for mice at all hours. At night, owls listen for mice rustling through leaves or grass so they can swoop down on them in the darkness. A captured mouse has little hope of escaping an owl's sharp claws.

These predators and others, such as snakes, skunks, weasels, coyotes, and hawks, help keep house mice populations from growing too large.

House mice have short life spans. Although they can live up to six years in captivity, wild house mice usually live only 15 to 18 months. Despite the many predators and the short life spans of mice, a colony can become overpopulated.

House mice can breed for the first time when they are between six and eight weeks old—just a few weeks after leaving the nest. After a female house mouse has given birth, she can become pregnant again in as little as two days, and have from 8 to 10 litters per year.

Outdoor house mice generally breed only from spring through fall, when the weather is warm and food is plentiful. In this short time, a female mouse is able to have about 5 litters. At an average rate of 7 pups per litter, it is easy to see how fast a mouse colony can grow.

But nature has more ways to keep the house mouse population down. As was mentioned earlier, only the chief buck mates in a large colony. In addition, the females in an overpopulated colony become less able to have young. The stress caused by overcrowding can cause a bodily change in female mice that makes them temporarily unable to give birth as often. This bodily state continues until the overcrowding ends and the population is back to a comfortable size.

While the house mouse is the mouse we may see most often, there are many other **species,** or kinds, of mice who inhabit outdoor areas throughout the western hemisphere.

Many species of deer mice, or white-footed mice, are found in North and South America—as far north as Alaska and as far south as Colombia. They can live almost anywhere—in deserts, swamps, forests, or grasslands. Deer mice are usually slightly larger than house mice and have brown or gray fur on top and white underbellies. Their big ears and bright black eyes give them an alert, intelligent expression. They generally feed at night, eating the seeds of many different plants.

As their name suggests, grasshopper mice eat insects, such as grasshoppers. They also kill and eat scorpions, worms, lizards, and even other mice. These little hunters are about the size of house mice or larger, with stocky bodies and short, thick tails. Northern grasshopper mice are buff colored on top and white underneath. Southern grasshopper mice are also white underneath but are brown or gray on top. These mice live in the dry areas and deserts of the western United States and northern Mexico.

American harvest mice live in the grassy areas of Canada, the United States, Mexico, and Central and South America. Some species are smaller than house mice and others are larger. Harvest mice are known for their climbing ability. They can scamper up and down tall, swaying stalks of grass, using their tails for balance and support. They prefer a diet of seeds and live in round nests woven of grasses. These nests are suspended from bushes or from other stalks of grass. Like most mice, harvest mice are brown or gray on top and white or pinkish white underneath.

"Meadow mice," or meadow voles, are the most common North American rodents. Voles are not actually mice, although they are like them in many ways. Unfortunately, not only are meadow voles the most common rodents, they are also the most destructive. Meadow voles have huge appetites and must eat their weight in food every day. They do great damage to plants while they are eating. The stout, short-tailed meadow voles are larger than house mice and have shaggy, dark brown fur. Meadow voles are found across North America.

Many people keep house mice as pets. Pet shops offer mice of various colors, like these. Their different colors and markings are the results of **selective breeding**. This means humans have controlled their mating to get pups with special colors of fur. No matter how different these mice look, they are all descendants of house mice.

Pet mice are playful and fascinating to watch. Bred "cage mice" behave like their wild relatives but are less shy. They may live as long as six years if they are well cared for.

The floor of a mouse cage should be covered with something clean and absorbent, like wood shavings. It is best to change these at least every two days to keep the mice comfortable and the cage from smelling. Mice also need to have some grass and hay in the cage for nest building.

Food bowls should be fixed and washable. Your mice will appreciate having these filled with grain seeds, grasses, rice, sunflower seeds, and similar foods. Prepared seed mixtures can be bought at pet stores. Mice also like leftovers, like hard stale bread, salad leaves, boiled potatoes, cucumbers, or raisins. Give them a piece of wood to gnaw on so they can keep their teeth sharp and short. Drinking water remains cleanest in a drinking trough designed for rodents.

Pet mice need a little sleeping house and an exercise wheel. In a cage, mice have no place to run, so the wheel lets them run all they want and need.

Finally, it is important to remember that pet mice, like their wild relatives, don't like to live alone. The cage that makes your mice happiest is the one large enough to house a small mouse colony.

We hope you've enjoyed your look through the mouse hole. The *Mus musculus* will probably never be everyone's most welcome guest. But as long as it can count on humans for food and shelter, this tiny creature will continue to make its home with us.

So the next time you hear a rustle in the night, cover your food and watch carefully—there might be a mouse in the house!

GLOSSARY

altricial: completely helpless at birth

amniotic sac: a membrane around some kinds of unborn animals that protects them before birth

burrow: a hole dug in the ground that is used for shelter

chief buck: the dominant male in a mouse colony

colony: mice that share the same territory

dormancy: a deep sleeplike state in which body functions slow down

hierarchy: members of a group that are ranked by levels of power and importance

hoard: to store large amounts of something

incisors: sharp front teeth

in heat: ready to mate

precocial: fairly independent at birth

pups: baby mice

rodent: the scientific order of small gnawing mammals that includes mice

selective breeding: the mating of chosen animals to produce offspring with desired characteristics

species: a group of plants or animals that share similar characteristics

sperm: male reproductive cells

tactile hairs: hairs, such as whiskers, that provide an animal with an added sense of touch

teats: a female mammal's nipples, from which young draw milk

territory: the area in which an animal lives and claims as its own

umbilical cord: a cord that connects a baby to its mother before birth and supplies the baby with the substances necessary to keep it alive

wean: to stop nursing

INDEX

ABOUT THE AUTHORS

Heiderose and Andreas Fischer-Nagel received degrees in biology from the University of Berlin. Their special interests include animal behavior, wildlife protection, and environmental control. The Fischer-Nagels have collaborated as authors and photographers on several internationally successful science books for children. They attribute the success of their books to their "love of children and of our threatened environment" and believe that "children learning to respect nature today are tomorrow's protectors of nature."

The Fischer-Nagels live in Germany with their daughters, Tamarica and Cosmea Désirée.

Additional photographs courtesy of: p. 5, Rita Summers/ Amwest Picture Agency; p. 29 (right), p. 36, p. 38 (left), p. 40, Dwight R. Kuhn Photography; p. 39 (top), C. Allan Morgan Photography.